Touching the Void

David Greig was born in Edinburgh. His plays include *Europe*, *The Architect*, *The Speculator*, *The Cosmonaut's Last Message to the Woman He Once Loved in the Former Soviet Union*, *Outlying Islands*, *San Diego*, *Pyrenees*, *The American Pilot*, *Yellow Moon*, *Damascus*, *Midsummer*, *Dunsinane*, *The Strange Undoing of Prudencia Hart*, *The Monster in the Hall*, *The Events* and *Lanark*. His translations and adaptations include Camus's *Caligula*, Euripides' *The Bacchae*, Strindberg's *Creditors*, J.M. Barrie's *Peter Pan* and Roald Dahl's *Charlie and the Chocolate Factory*. In 1990 he co-founded Suspect Culture with Graham Eatough to produce collaborative, experimental theatre work. Since 2016 he has been Artistic Director of the city's Royal Lyceum Theatre.

Joe Simpson is the author of several best-selling books, of which the first, *Touching the Void*, won both the NCR award and the Boardman Tasker Award. His later books are *This Game of Ghosts* – the sequel to *Touching the Void* – *Storms of Silence*, *Dark Shadows Falling*, *The Beckoning Silence* and two novels, *The Water People* and *The Sound of Gravity*.

also by David Greig

OUTLYING ISLANDS
SAN DIEGO
PYRENEES
THE AMERICAN PILOT
YELLOW MOON
DAMASCUS
MIDSUMMER (A PLAY WITH SONGS)
DUNSINANE
THE STRANGE UNDOING OF PRUDENCIA HART
THE MONSTER IN THE HALL
THE EVENTS

SELECTED PLAYS 1999–2009
(*San Diego, Outlying Islands, Pyrenees, The American Pilot,
Being Norwegian, Kyoto, Brewers Fayre*)

adaptations
CAMUS'S CALIGULA
EURIPIDES' THE BACCHAE
AUGUST STRINDBERG'S CREDITORS
LANARK

with Suspect Culture
CASANOVA

Published by Methuen

DAVID GREIG PLAYS: I
(*Europe, The Architect, The Cosmonaut's Last Message
to the Woman He Once Loved in the Former Soviet Union*)

VICTORIA

DAVID GREIG

Touching the Void

stage adaptation based on the book by

JOE SIMPSON

FABER & FABER

First published in 2018
by Faber and Faber Limited
The Bindery, 51 Hatton Garden,
London ECIN 8HN

Typeset by Country Setting, Kingsdown, Kent CT14 8ES
Printed in England by CPI Group (UK) Ltd, Croydon, Surrey CRO 44Y

The right of David Greig to be identified as author of this work
has been asserted in accordance with Section 77 of the Copyright,
Designs and Patents Act 1988

Touching the Void by Joe Simpson
was first published in 1988 by Jonathan Cape.

A CIP record for this book is available from the British Library

ISBN 978–0–571–35224–1

Printed and bound in the UK on FSC® certified paper in line with our continuing
commitment to ethical business practices, sustainability and the environment.
For further information see faber.co.uk/environmental-policy

8 10 9

A Note on Truth and Fiction

This play is a mythic reading of a real event which impacted on the lives of three real people. For that reason I would like to be up front about which parts of this text are 'true' and which are 'made up'. Our telling of the climb and accident on Siula Grande is based squarely on the story Joe Simpson told in the book, but we have made some elisions of time. For storytelling economy, we shortened the number of days the boys spent on the mountain. Also, Joe made two bivouacs on the journey from the glacier, not one. More significantly, in order to tell our version of the story, we have invented two characters. The character of Sarah is based on Joe's sister Sarah, as she is described in *This Game of Ghosts*, but apart from that initial inspiration she is our invention. Sadly, the real Sarah Simpson died some years ago and so we were not able to chat to her about her portrayal. Joe, however, indicated that he thinks Sarah might have enjoyed the thought of being portrayed in the play and he has kindly given us permission to use her name. Richard in this play is also a literary invention. The real Richard Hawking had many adventures in Uganda, South America and later in Sudan. Far from the bookish fanboy we portray, he was a man of action. Our Richard would probably have liked to have been him. Our Richard, a naive armchair adventurer with dreams of being a writer, is based, if anything, on me. Nevertheless, Richard has also kindly allowed us to use his name for the play.

David Greig
September 2018

Touching the Void, based on the book by Joe Simpson and adapted by David Greig, was a Bristol Old Vic, Royal Lyceum Theatre, Edinburgh, Royal & Derngate, Northampton, and Fuel co-production. It was first performed at the Bristol Old Vic on 8 September 2018. The cast, in alphabetical order, was as follows:

Sarah Fiona Hampton
Simon Edward Hayter
Richard Patrick McNamee
Joe Josh Williams

Director Tom Morris
Designer Ti Green
Lighting Designer Chris Davey
Composer and Sound Designer Jon Nicholls
Movement Director Sasha Milavic Davies
Casting Director Jill Green CDG

Characters

Joe

Sarah

Simon

Richard

Note

Text in ***italicised bold*** indicates choric speech

.

TOUCHING THE VOID

'We rope up at the cave, tying our fates together
for the day. A gesture of trust and solidarity,
marriage by a forty-foot length of polypropylene'

Andrew Greig, *Summit Fever*
(Edinburgh, 1997)

Act One

Inside the crevasse, a climber lies broken on a ledge of snow.

Joe SIMON!
Simon
simon
simon

A lovely stone church.
The congregation sing a shaky 'Rock of Ages'.
As they finish –
Sarah takes the pulpit.

Sarah Hello.
God, there's a lot of you!
Lots of Goretex.
Lots of climbers.
I'm Sarah, Joe's sister. Big sis.
I'm supposed to give the eulogy.
People say, don't they, on these occasions . . . 'Well, at least he died doing something he loved.'
Because Joe loved climbing, didn't he.
'At least he died doing something he loved.'
But that's bullshit, isn't it.
Because Joe wasn't climbing when he died, was he?
He was trapped inside a glacier
Alone.
And I think he would have hated that.
I'm sorry. That's all I have to say.
Oh, and just for the record, he didn't believe in God and he didn't like hymns.

Jameson's, a double.

She clicks her fingers.
    Music: Joy Division: 'Love Will Tear Us Apart'.
    A pub forms around Sarah.
    A climbers' bar.
    Jukebox, pool table, photos and memorabilia on the wall.
    It's the afternoon.
    The bar is empty.
    Sarah sways to the music from the jukebox.
    Her eyes closed.
    Simon enters, dressed smartly, in a black suit.
    He watches her for a moment.
    The music stops.
    She opens her eyes.

Sarah Simon?

Simon Yes.

A moment.

Sarah Thank you for coming.
    I'm sorry there isn't sandwiches.
    You would expect sandwiches at a wake.
    I probably forgot.

Simon Sarah, I'm sorry.

He reaches out to take her hand – they nearly touch.
    They're interrupted by Richard.
    Richard enters.

Richard Simon!

He has climbing rope around his shoulder, and he carries a walking axe.
    On his back, a jaunty backpack.

So this is it.
    The world famous Clachaig Inn!

Richard is out of breath.

Sorry I'm late.
   Directions and –
   Simon – you didn't say this place was in Scotland!
   Typical climber –
   'Bit of a slope, Richard!' – Turns out it's a bloody cliff.
   Or in Peru – 'Nice day out in the hills,' they said.
   A man died!
   Any sandwiches? I'm starving!

A moment.

I'm Richard.

Simon Richard, this is –

Richard Sarah, Joe's sister. Pleased to meet you.
   Well, when I say 'pleased' I'd rather your brother
wasn't dead, obviously, but you know what I mean.
   Sorry.

Sarah It's fine.

Simon Things must be –

Sarah Overwhelming –

Richard Overwhelming.
   I haven't been to many funerals.

Sarah Not a climber then?

Richard No.

Sarah I'm sorry, who are you?

Richard Richard.
   I don't really have a second name, or at least, Joe
could never remember it.
   I was with Joe and Simon on the expedition in Peru.
   Base-camp manager.

Simon We met Richard in Lima. He's travelling round the world.

Richard Gap year.

Simon Richard looked after our tents when we were up on the hill.

Richard I wasn't really interested in climbing before Peru but now, after everything that's happened, I've become obsessed. I've been reading all about it.

I am, what you might call, an armchair mountaineer.

Richard takes books out of his backpack.
He slaps them out on the table.

Mallory, Tenzing, *The North Face of the Eiger* . . .
It's an absolutely extraordinary world.

Simon It's not really.

Sarah Isn't it?

Simon It's just a hobby.

Richard I've become so obsessed with climbing I'm actually thinking of writing a book.

Simon About climbing?
A memoir about the Siula Grande expedition.
The story of an ordinary young man accidentally caught up in an extraordinary mountain drama.

Simon Sitting in a tent at base camp?

Richard No. Well, a bit. But really it's about how in different ways, you, Joe and me were all climbers on Siula Grande . . . each of us reaching for the heights of life, risking our lives, not me obviously, to escape the earthly complications of being human . . .

I'm going to call it
Avoiding the Touch.

A great moan comes from the void – the pub shakes.
They lose footing for a second.
    Then it's fine.

Would you like a drink, Sarah?

Sarah looks at her whisky glass, there's still a measure
in it.
    She swigs it.
    Finishes it.

Sarah Jameson's. A bottle. No ice.

Richard leaves to get her drink.

This is a climbers' pub, isn't it? Didn't Joe and you used
to come here?

Simon Sometimes.

Sarah Is this where you planned the expedition?

Simon No.

Sarah Where was that?

Simon That was a bar in the Alps, I think.
    In Chamonix. It had tables like this though, with
tablecloths.
    The Clachaig doesn't have tablecloths.

Sarah takes out a hip flask.
    She takes a swig.
    Offers some to Simon.

Sarah Let's drink.
    More drink.

Simon takes it, swigs.

I want to drink hard.

Sudden rip of cold – wind – supernatural – heartbeat.
The void – asserts itself.

Simon Funerals are strange.

Sarah Joe would have hated it.
   All the fussing and the handshakes and God.
   He would have hated God.

Simon And being polite.

Sarah Yeah.

   A moment.

Sarah Fortunately for Joe, you don't have to be polite if
you're the deceased.
   If you're the deceased, you can be as rude as you like.
   You don't even have to bother to fucking turn up.
   Just can just disappear into a glacier and never come
back.
   Very rude.
   Bastard.

   A moment.

Simon Look, Sarah, I didn't really know Joe that well.
We were just –

Sarah I know –

Simon *and* **Sarah** Climbing partners.

Sarah Just.

   A moment.

I hate climbers.
   Fucking climbers . . .
   Fucking anoraks, fucking fleeces, fucking carabiners,
fucking trousers,
   Fucking wiry little French wankers hogging the
jukebox all night . . .
   And fucking stories.
   Fucking endless fucking stories about how they nearly
died

8

Blah blah epic blah
You know what climbers are?

Simon No?

Sarah Climbers are cunts.

A moment.

Sorry.

Simon It's all right.
I don't think the sister of the deceased has to be polite at a funeral either.

Sarah I actually –

Richard enters with drinks.

Richard Sorry, sorry, took ages to find the bar, ended up in Switzerland.

They sit at a table.

Cheers.

Sarah *and* **Simon** Cheers.

Richard sits.

Richard Sarah,
I hope you don't mind.
We brought you some of Joe's things. Things he left in his tent. We thought you might want them.

Richard opens his backpack, takes out a crumpled poly bag.
She looks through it.

His passport. Some money. A book he was reading.
Some photos I took on the trip. I made copies. There's not many.

Sarah Is this it?

Richard Yeah.

Sarah It doesn't seem much evidence of a life.

Simon No.

Richard Were you very close?

Sarah I used to torture him.

Richard I see.

Sarah Get him to do things, steal sweets, ride his bike down stairs, jump out of trees – he had a thick skull, Joe, you could hit it off rocks and he'd still stand up, lip quivering, refusing to cry. It was funny. Always funny.

Simon hands Sarah an envelope.

What's this?

Simon A letter.

Richard We found it with his money.

Simon It's addressed to you.

Richard Wrapped in a little plastic bag, under a stone.

Simon He hid it when we left to climb the hill.

Richard Took us hours and hours and hours to find it.

Simon He showed me the hiding place but I forgot.

Richard Typical Simon, always somewhere else.
   Aren't you going to read it?

Sarah No.

A moment.

There's something I want to ask you.
   Both of you.
   It might seem a bit odd.
   It is odd

But I feel I have to ask
Is that okay?

Simon Of course.

Richard You can ask anything.

Sarah Are you absolutely sure he's dead?

A moment.

I mean, are you certain?
Are you one hundred per cent certain that Joe's dead?
There's no chance at all that he could have survived?
That he's still out there?
I mean, there isn't a body.

Simon He fell from an ice cliff.

Richard 'Fell'.

Simon Into a crevasse.

Richard Even if he had survived the fall –

Simon He wouldn't survive the fall.
He already had a broken leg
And a shattered ankle,
He was dehydrated and hypothermic,
He wouldn't have been able to climb out.
I'm sorry.

Sarah It just doesn't *feel* like he's dead.
It feels like he's just left the room, gone to get a drink at the bar
Put a record on the jukebox
Nipped off for a piss – or . . .
I dream about him.

Simon Sarah, I know it's hard but –

Sarah But what?

Simon You have to accept.

Sarah Accept?

Simon Joe's gone.
  You need to let him go.

Sarah What, like you did?

  A moment.

I don't want to let him go.
  I want to bring him back.
  I want to put him back together in my head
  And right now I can't.
  I can't
  Because right now I have no fucking idea
  What happened to him.
  He's just gone.

Simon We were on an ice cliff –

Sarah Why?

Richard Simon was attempting a rescue –

Sarah Why?

Simon Joe had broken his leg?

Sarah No. No. No.
  Not that why.

  *Sudden rips of cold – wind – supernatural – heartbeat.
    The void – asserts itself.*

Why do you do it?

Simon Do what?

Sarah Climb mountains?

Richard Because they're there.

Sarah I'm not asking you. I'm asking him.

Simon It's hard to explain.

Sarah Try.

Simon The exercise. The outdoors. It's a friendly crowd.

Sarah Those are reasons you take up Morris dancing.
      I'm asking why you do something that has you
hanging off cliffs thousands of feet up. I'm talking about
going to places you can never get rescued from? Why do
you do that?

Richard In 1928 a journalist asked George Mallory why
he wanted to climb Everest, Mallory said, 'Because it's
there.'

Sarah I heard you the first time, Professor Yaffle.

Richard It's just that, for a lot of climbers, Mallory's
answer is their answer.

Sarah What happened to Mallory, then?

Simon He died.

Sarah How?

Richard On Everest. He fell near the summit.

Sarah That must have been confusing. One minute
Everest was there. Next minute it wasn't. 'Ahhhh . . .'
Then, 'Ouch', it was there again. A bit too fucking there.
      Sorry. Is that in bad taste?
      What can I say? My brother's dead. I lost my moral
compass. Do you happen to have one? Oh no, you're
a climber.
      I know the mountain was there.
      The mountain's always been there.
      What I want to know is why were you there?
      Why were you on the side of a fucking mountain in
the first place?
      That's what I don't understand.
      Why do you fucking do it?

An assertion of the void.
  Wind, cold, a roar . . . of determination.

Simon It started when I was a kid. I hated school. I
always wanted to be outside. Then one day I saw some
lads bouldering on a crag. I tried it. I was good at it.
  I'm no good with books. I can't play football.
  In every other part of my life I was ungainly. But on
the crags I felt like I'd come home.
  I was . . . gainly.
  It's a feeling, I can't really explain it.

Sarah Show me then.

Simon Now just look at the stone in front of you,
  Look for a hold.
  That's it.
  Now look for a placement for your foot.

She does so.

Feel the lip of the hold.
  Do you feel it?
  Grip with your fingers.
  Now search again with your foot.
  It might be easier with your shoes off –
  Feel the rock
  Find the hold
  Search
  Touch
  Pull.

Simon / Sarah Yes!

Sarah looks for another hold.

Sarah Now I'm lost.

Simon Look at the face
  Find a weakness
  Look for a shadow
  Feel the shape of the rock.

14

Sarah Okay.
  Okay.
  Got it!

She continues her climb.

You still haven't answered my question.

Simon Haven't I?

Sarah You've told me about being a kid – you've told me about cragging – warm summer days in England. But what I want to know is – why mountains? Why go somewhere where you're doing this – but on a 4,000-foot cliff in a blizzard and a thousand miles from help?

Simon You really want to know?

Sarah I really want to know.

Simon All right –

*Suddenly we're on the West Face of an Alp.
  Wind – snow.*

Sarah What the fuck?!

Simon Don't look down!

Sarah screams. Simon laughs.

You're all right – I've got you.

Sarah Take me back take me back take me back!

Simon Breathe
  Focus on the rock
  Everything's the same as before
  Only now we're higher
  Hold
  Breathe
  You okay?

Sarah Okay.

Simon Good.
Now copy me.

They start to climb together – in parallel.

Hit – hold – hit – hold.
Kick – push – kick – breathe.
Hit – hold – hit – hold.
Kick – push – kick – breathe.

Sarah Where are we now?

Simon Climbing the Walker Spur of the Grandes Jorasses in the French Alps
Few years ago.
I'm climbing with Joe.

Joe appears.

We've only just met.
You're Joe.

Sarah What?

Simon Do you ever think it's weird, Joe?
Doing this for fun.

Joe What?

Sarah Joe?

Joe Launching yourself up the side of an Alp at extreme risk to life and limb?

Simon Yeah, that.
Why do you think you do it?

Joe I dunno.
I see a line and I want to try it
I want to be up there
Moving across steep ground
Getting into a rhythm
Pick the right line

On the right hill.
You lose yourself completely,
In the blink of an eye a whole day's gone.
It's like dancing.

Simon Not the way you climb, mate.

Joe Fuck off.

Simon You climb like a robot attacking a wall.

Joe You don't get a prize for pretty.

Simon Do you need more rope?

Joe Please.
The thing is, I just think the question's wrong. When people ask, why do you climb, the question assumes that it's being here, clambering up rocks, that's weird. But it isn't climbing that's weird – it's *not* climbing. Climbing's what humans *do*. Have done for a hundred thousand years – it's what we did since before we were human – since we were just apes –

Joe sets up a belay.

We evolved to put our hands on stone or branches and feel for a hold to pull ourselves up – just look at any kid – any girl or boy in a playground – on a wall in the street – what are they doing? Climbing.
Climb when ready!

Simon Climbing!

Joe belays as Simon and Sarah climb.

Joe It's not climbing that's weird, it's normal life – living in captivity – doing a job – sitting at a desk – lying on a couch with dead eyes watching Esther Rantzen – it's jogging – it's mortgages – polyester shirts and shiny jackets and kissing the arse of a twenty-year-old with a clipboard – bosses and underlings – houses and cars –

small talk and bullshit – it's civilisation – that's what's
nuts – that's what's weird. Not why climb, but why not?
    Why live like that
    When you can live like this?

Simon and Sarah have made it to the ledge.

Simon / Sarah (*simultaneously*) Yes.

Simon Another pitch?

Richard Can I come?

Sarah No!

Simon / Sarah We need someone to look after base camp.

Climbing a pitch on the Grandes Jorasses
A thousand foot up – a thousand to go
A hundred feet above the last ice screw
Fifteen more feet till the safety of snow

Hit – hold – hit – hold
Kick – push – kick – breathe
Hit – hold – hit – hold
Kick – push – kick – breathe.

Sarah Whoh! Shit.

Screw in an ice screw – find some protection
On the back of your neck you can feel the sun
Read the face of the rock, you speak this language.
Hand, ice, axe, breath, water, air, become one.

Hit – hold – hit – hold
Kick – push – kick – breathe
Hit – hold – hit – hold
Kick – push – kick – breathe.

Sarah Jesus.

Simon Don't look down. Now look down!
    If we fall now – we'll fall for a minute,

Rip out the ice screw then spin into air
Kicking our legs in the void in the silence,
Screaming a scream that no one will hear.

Sarah looks down.

Sarah Oh my God. I feel sick.

Simon It's okay.
It's okay.
It's only the void.

Simon helps her.

The trick with the void is not to fear it.
But to accept it – inhale it – use it to concentrate.
Use it like a drug to heighten your awareness –
sharpen your senses.
The void doesn't want to hurt you.
The void's just there.

The void's our companion – the void climbs beside us.
Life with the void is life times a thousand.

They reach the ledge.
Joe has gone.
Simon helps Sarah unclip.
She sits beside him and looks out.
We're back in the pub.

Sarah Okay,
That was good.
That was helpful.
Now take me back to the start.

Richard The start of what?

Sarah You and Joe, the expedition to Peru, the accident,
everything.
Tell me everything,
I need to get it clear.

Richard It started in Peru –

Simon It started in the Alps.
There's a scrap of waste ground on the outskirts of Chamonix
Which is a kind of makeshift campsite where young climbers come from all around Europe,
Gather for the summer
Looking to make a name for themselves
With not much more than a sleeping bag and the price of a cable-car fare to get them to the start of the glaciers.

Richard Simon didn't even have a sleeping bag.

Simon One night I met Joe
Round a campfire sharing a tin of shoplifted beans.
We'd both thrown ourselves up a few routes separately but this night we thought why not team up together and take on Mont Blanc?
Joe fancied an unusual route, it had been done before – but it was . . .
Interestingly difficult
In fact it nearly got him killed, but in the end, we did it and left the two of us walking into Chamonix that night feeling –

Joe We can do this!

Simon We can fucking do it!

Joe We make a good team.

Simon So –

Joe What we need now is a new route –

Simon A big new route –

Joe On a proper mountain.

Simon Over five thousand metres.

Joe Alps again?

Simon No, not the Alps, all the good routes in the Alps have been done.

Joe Himalayas?

Simon Summit permit too expensive.

Joe Where then?

Simon The Andes.

Simon shows Joe some maps and plans.

Cordillera Huayhuash.

Joe Never heard of it.

Simon Seven big hills in the middle of Peru . . . Fly in to Lima.

Joe Rent a llama.

Simon Bus to Cajatambo.

Joe Do you hear the drums, Fernando?

Simon Acclimatise for a week or so.

Joe Beer

Simon Rent donkeys

Joe Nice ass

Simon Get the gear up to base camp and there it is –

He shows Joe an illustration.

Siula Grande.

Joe Fucking hell.

Sarah Fucking hell.

Richard Fucking hell.

All It's beautiful.

Simon And . . . there's an unclimbed route on the West Face
From there, to there, to there . . . and back down. See?

They all look.

We can save up over winter, fly out next summer. What do you say?

Joe I dunno, Si.
It means getting a crap job for a whole year just for money. It means another year of sacrificing everything to climbing. It means another year of walking further and further away from normal life and getting deeper and deeper into this big mountain shit.

Simon So what do you say?

Joe Yes.
I say,
Fuck yes.

Sudden change of atmosphere.
South American music on the jukebox.

Sarah Where are we now?

Richard Bar El Poco, Lima.

Sarah For a supposedly outdoor pursuit, an awful lot of climbing seems to take place in bars.

Richard This is where they meet me –

They shake hands.

I was just going round South America, backpacking, you know, staying in hostels, eating in street bars, just what everybody does, making a bit of money busking, mostly Simon and Garfunkel.

I'd fallen in with an old Peruvian guy who played the pan pipes. I think he maybe sold hash as well. Anyway, he took me to this bar and I saw these two British guys wearing brightly coloured outdoor jackets, you know, the crispy, crunchy ones that make a noise. Most backpackers go round in a stinky vest and a pair of clown trousers so I could tell these guys weren't backpackers but they weren't tourists either – they were something else.

By the way, that's how my book's going to begin.

Sarah Just get on with the story.

Richard So, I asked them . . .
Are you climbers?

Joe Climbers, yeah,

Richard Are you here on an expedition?

Simon That's right, yeah.

Richard Where are you going?

Simon Siula Grande.

Richard I don't know that one.

Simon Not many people do.
It's quite remote.

Richard Is it hard?

Joe It's got its charms.

Simon Bit of a cheeky one.

Richard That's the way they spoke. That's how climbers speak.

Joe It's a stroll in the hills.

Simon Frisky day out.

Richard It's like a special language. Everything's not really what it is.

Anyway, shared my spliff with them and they bought me a beer.

So why do you want to climb Siula Grande? Is it the highest in the Andes?

Simon Not the highest, no.

Richard But it's famous?

Simon Not really.

Joe We're going to go up the face.

Simon Direct.

Joe See?

Simon Nobody's ever done that before.

Richard And I suppose, if you manage this one you can always move on to a bigger one next time?

Simon Yeah.

Joe If we manage.

Richard And I suppose if you make it. One day you might be able to take on Everest!

Simon / Joe Everest?

Simon Mate –

Joe We're not backpackers.

Richard At the time I didn't get that joke but now I do. It's funny because Everest's actually –

Simon interrupts.

Simon What about you, Richard, anyway? What brings you to Peru?

Richard I'm looking for material for my novel.

Joe You're a writer?

Richard Just starting out, bit like you guys.

Joe And you're writing a novel?

Richard Novel. Novella. Memoir. I'm not sure. Possibly an interlinked series of short stories.

Joe What's it about?

Richard I don't know.

...

The trouble is, nothing's happened to me yet. At least, nothing that seems worth writing about. I got felt up by a policeman in Caracas. But, apart from that . . . nada . . . I really need something to happen or else the book's going to be shit.

Simon Why don't you come with us?

Richard Me? I can't climb. I get dizzy in a lift.

Simon Not on the hill – come to base camp,
Couple of days on buses, three-day walk-in
To look after the tents.
Base-camp manager.

A moment.

Richard All right.
I can read. I can write. I can do my yoga.
It'll be an adventure!

*Base camp . . . Richard sets up the tent.
Simon and Joe lay out their equipment.*

Joe Rope

Simon Carabiners

Joe Pitons

Simon Ice screws

Joe Crampons times four.

Richard Joe and Simon are making their ascent *in Alpine style.*

Sarah What does that mean?

Joe Snow stakes.

Richard In early days, climbing big mountains meant expeditions with porters, and fixed ropes and oxygen, and camps high up the hill – hundreds of people all there to get two men on the summit. They call that 'siege climbing' –

Simon Ice axes times two.

Richard To climb Alpine style means doing away with all of that.

Joe Still too much gear.

Richard Alpine style goes back to basics.
    Two people and a rope.

Simon Stoves times two.

Joe Dried food.

Richard Go light, go fast, carry everything you need.

Simon Tea.

Joe Biscuits?

Simon Chocolate digestives.

Richard Alpine style means peeling away the layers that come between you and a direct line to the top of the mountain.

Joe Tent?

Simon Too heavy
    We'll bivvy in snow holes.

Richard Just two men, a rope and the abyss.

Joe Gas – one, two, three . . . how many?

Richard It's beautiful.

Simon Two days up, two days down I reckon
    Three nights. If the weather holds
    Three cans should do it.
    Four to be safe.

Richard It's also very dangerous.

The boys pack their rucksacks.

Joe You scared?

Simon A bit

Joe Still

Simon Still

Joe It's no fun unless you're scared a bit.

Simon gets into his climbing gear.

Okay.

Simon I think that's us.

Joe I think it is.

Sarah Like Toni Kurz.

Richard Yes!

Sarah Joe told me about him.

Joe Toni Kurz is my hero.
    He did all the most difficult climbs but he did them
simply.
    Kurz was Austrian, in the 1930s he and his mate
Andreas Hinterstoisser climbed all over the Alps – put up
new routes everywhere, together they basically invented
Alpine style.

Sarah What happened to him?

Joe He died.

27

Sarah I knew it – I knew it – I knew he'd die.

They always fucking do in these stories.

Climbers.

Joe No, sis, the point isn't *that* he died the point is *how* he died!

One summer they decided to cycle from Germany to Switzerland and take on the last great unclimbed wall –

The North Face of the Eiger.

Everyone thought it was impossible.

They set off one perfect afternoon.

A third of the way up they met two Austrians trying for the face as well, Willi Angerer and Edi Rainer. These guys were good too so the four of them decided to team up and make an attempt together.

In the cafés in the village below the face, a crowd gathered to watch.

For four days the boys climbed – little dots on a wall of rock – flies on the side of a house – up and up – dancing past places where climbers had failed before, and they nearly made it.

Sarah So what happened?

Joe High up near the summit Willi Angerer got hit on the head by a falling rock. He was badly injured so they were forced to climb down. Downclimbing is more dangerous than climbing up. You have to reverse all your moves – it took them too long and on the fifth day they got caught in an avalanche. Hinterstoisser disappeared. Rainer was pulled off the cliff. His rope caught Angerer and strangled him.

Only Toni Kurz is left alive, dangling over an over-hanging cliff.

Rescuers from the village manage to get very close to him. But they can't reach him. Their ropes aren't long enough.

He hangs there all night, alone.

His right hand freezes solid.

He can't climb up or down.

He can't even cut the rope and try his luck in a fall because of his frozen hand.

There's nothing the rescuers can do.

Toni! Toni! Toni!

There's only forty feet between them and a crowd of thousands in the cafés watching it all through binoculars but it doesn't matter how many people could see him – Toni Kurz was all alone.

And he fought . . . he fought and he fought

He survived a whole night hanging, he climbed the rope one handed, he untangled the rope into the three strands to make it longer, he climbed, he cursed, he tried, he hung.

He fought

Until he couldn't fight any more.

And he turned

And said to them

Soft and clear as a night bell

'Ich kann nicht mehr'

Joe I can't go on.

Beautiful.

Sarah No, Joe, not beautiful.

Ugly.

Horrible

Ugly and cold

But you love it, don't you

You love it because no matter who you climb with

You always tie Death in on the other end of your rope.

Because it's no fun climbing without him, is it?

Joe? Joe? Joe?

A roar from the void – a moan – cold.

Simon Are you okay?

Sarah Show me the mountain.

A moment.
    The boys are packed and ready.

Simon All right.

Sarah and Joe watch as Simon and Richard create the geography with the available resources.
    Simon moves a table.

This is Siula Grande.

He takes the tablecloth off the table so it hangs to make a west face.

The west face is about 4,500 foot high.

He moves another pub table.
    Joins the tablecloth to another pub table to make a ridge.

Under the face is a glacier, which runs down into the valley.
    Base camp is just under a ridge beneath two glacial lakes.

Richard This is base camp.

He moves his pile of climbing books to a place a distance away.

This is me.

He puts a peanut down on the books.

Simon On the first day of the climb we walk in past these lakes. Up through the rocky valley for approximately six miles.

Richard I came with them. It was *really* tiring.

Simon You have to remember, before we even start, we're already as high as Mont Blanc.

Richard Breathing feels like you're trying to suck air out of a stone.

Simon The first real climbing obstacle is here –

Richard A steep cliff of ice and rock with constant stonefall –

Simon Joe called it Bomb Alley.

Richard That's where I turned back.
  Then they picked their way over another mile or so of moraines, it's really difficult walking over moraines, they're big heaps of rock all piled up in a mess like spilt Lego, but eventually they reached the glacier itself. The glacier was only one and a half a miles long but it took ages to cross because it's basically a maze of huge crevasses.
  Crossing a glacier is always dangerous, but Simon and Joe know what they're doing. They've done it in the Alps loads of times before. It's tense but they make it fine. The plan is to climb up the face and bivvy high; round about here. They're aiming for this rising rock ramp which will take us to a couloir.

Richard Funnel.

Sarah Right.

Richard Just beneath the summit ridge. That's where they'll bivvy again, before traversing to the summit on the last day. Then back down along the ridge to the col . . . across the crevasses of the glacier, over the moraines, through Bomb Alley, past the lakes and to base camp in time for tea.
  That's the plan.

He puts two peanuts on the face.

That's Simon.
  That's Joe.

Joe Climb!

Simon Climbing.

Richard It's five p.m. on the first day – they're up at around two thousand feet – Jesus! – they've spent the whole day climbing up a huge wall of rock and ice and now they're heading for a funnel which will take them up to a rock ramp tomorrow – with a bit of luck – on to the summit. Bellow them is the yawning void – two thousand feet of teetering emptiness dragging them towards it – my palms are sweating just looking at them.

> *Simon and Joe climb.*
> *They fall into a rhythm.*
> *Sun rises over them.*
> *The sound of ice.*
> *The metal of their protection clinks.*
> *They move across the rock smoothly.*

Sarah . . .

Richard Feel.

Sarah They look happy.

Richard Don't they.

Sarah Lost.

Richard They're breaking new ground – putting up a new route – risking everything for the ultimate prize

Sarah The summit.

Richard Two lines in the *British Alpine Journal* – 'Siula Grande. West Face, Simpson and Yates (1983).'

Sarah Is that it?

Richard Well, I suppose there might be a photograph as well.

Simon Climb when ready.

Joe Climbing.

Sarah Fucking hell.

Richard What?

Sarah All this death for two lines in a climbing magazine.

Richard Well, it's slightly more than a magazine.

Sarah takes the magazine.

Sarah Show me the entry.

Richard It's not there.

Sarah What do you mean it's not there?

Richard Well, to claim a route, you have to get back alive.

A moment.

Sarah Where are they now?

Richard points –

Richard Eleven a.m. on day two. Here.

Joe and Simon high up on the west face.
It is high altitude.
The sound of light wind, rockfall and the tinkle of ice.
Sun beats down on them.

Joe I can't find any fucking protection.

Richard He's trying to get one of these into the rock and putting the rope through it so when you fall, it catches you.

Right now he's roped to Simon who's belaying him. The higher he climbs without protection further he'll fall if he makes a mistake. The further he falls the more chance he'll rip Simon off the hill with him.

Sarah What would happen then?

Richard Okay. This peanut is Joe. If Joe falls and Simon's protection doesn't hold. It'll take him eighteen seconds to hit the glacier . . . Count it.

Joe Fuck.

Richard makes the peanut fall, slowly, off the table onto the floor.

One, two, three –
    There goes Simon –
    Four, five, six, seven, eight, nine, ten, eleven, twelve, thirteen, fourteen, fifteen, sixteen, seventeen, eighteen –
    Splat – two – three – splat.

Sarah Mate.

Joe Safe.

They reach a ledge.

Simon What time is it?

Joe Lunchtime.

Simon Not bad.

Joe We started late.

Simon Ten and a half pitches in four and a half hours.

Joe We're going to finish this thing, you know.

Simon Not if we can't get past those seracs.

Joe Oh.

The check out the route ahead.

Simon What do you think?

Joe It looks hard. That right side looks as if it's blocked by big icicles. The left is horrible climbing but at least it's rock.

Simon I'll try the rock.

Simon climbs.
  He puts a cam in a crack.
  He gingerly tests with his feet.
  Then his hand.
  He climbs.
  Joe tightens the belay.
  Quite a long time.

Watch me!
  Shit.
  I'm gonna go I'm gonna go I'm gonna go!

Suddenly rock gives way. Simon falls –
  Joe catches Simon on the rope almost immediately.

Joe Fuck!

They recover.
  Joe laughs.

Your face.

Simon I was sure that was solid.

Joe We'll have to try the other way.

Simon You try. I'm knackered.

Joe All right . . . but watch out . . . When I'm going up I'm going to have to knock those icicles away. Some of them look fucking big.

Simon Just shout.

Joe starts climbing.
  He hits his ice axe hard into the ice.
  Bunny-hops on his crampons.
  Finally Joe stops climbing.
  He fixes himself into position.
  He waves his axe to knock the icicles away.
  A rain of ice showers down on both of them.

Ow! Shit!

Joe Fuck. Balls. Tits.

> *Simon and Joe cower under a barrage of ice.*
>   *Then it's over.*

Simon Christ, Joe! You were supposed to shout.

Joe Sorry, I didn't think.

Simon Fucking hell.

> *Joe is injured.*

Your mouth is bleeding.

Joe My own fault.
Simon.

Simon What?

Joe Look.

Simon What?
Oh
Fuck.

> *The pub shifts and heaves like a ship sinking.*
>   *The void groans.*
>   *Ice and wind.*

Sarah What can they see?

Joe Snow.

Simon Shit.

Sarah Is snow bad?

Richard It's not good. Climbers like rock and ice. Hard things. Snow's soft. It won't hold you. Snow hides the rocks. It can avalanche. It looks solid but it isn't. In the Alps at this height you don't tend to get much snow. But the Andes have a different weather system.

Joe It's like fucking candyfloss.

Simon Let's stop. Let's rest.
It's too late in the day.
My hands are fucked, I'm frozen.

Joe Okay.
We'll dig a snow hole here.
Go for the summit in the morning.

Richard goes over to the jukebox.
Puts in a quid.
Music: 'This is the Day'.

Richard You literally dig out a hole in the snow and use it like an igloo.

Joe and Simon build a snow hole.
  As they build, night falls.

Sarah It must be freezing?

Richard No, it's warm. It keeps out the wind and snow's a good insulator. That's why you find piles of it lasting weeks on the pavement after a snowfall.

Sarah and Richard get in the snow cave with Simon and Joe.

Joe Brew?

Simon Ta.

Joe hands Simon a flask of tea.

Joe That's the last of the gas.

Simon We'll be down tomorrow.

They look out at the view.

Joe Look at that.

Simon I know.

Joe Moonlight over the Andes.

Simon So many mountains.

A moment.

Joe Simon –?

Simon What?

Joe Nobody else has ever seen this.

Simon No.

Joe It's just us.

Simon Just us.

A moment.

Sarah It really is beautiful.

Richard Isn't it – but –

Sarah But what?

Simon Roll us a fag, will you.

Joe I gave up, mate.

Simon I know. But there's tobacco and papers in my rucksack. Would you mind rolling me one?

Joe Is it my superior rolling technique?

Simon No.

Joe What then?

Simon Fingers are a bit stiff.

Sarah Frostbite.

Richard Two middle fingers.

Joe Shit.

Richard Everything in climbing weighs an advantage against a risk.

Climbing without tents saves weight so you move faster up the hill but snow caves take a lot of digging.

The boys are cosy now but it took them two hours to build that cave.

In that two hours, they got very cold.

That has a consequence.

Simon We'll be at the summit tomorrow.
Should be fine.

Joe What then?

Simon We get back down.

Joe That's not what I meant.

Simon What do you mean?

They share the fag.

Joe I just mean . . . we've given months of our lives for this moment. And now we're here. At the top of a new route in the Andes. But by the time we're back down there on to the glacier we'll have already started to forget. We'll be dreaming of the next hill; a harder one, a higher one. I can already feel it . . . a hunger, a great mountain-shaped void. We're supposed to be healthy outdoors types, you and me, but do you never think to yourself . . . this is just another addiction. If it wasn't a mountain, we'd have to get this from bank robberies, we'd have to get it from fucking heroin.

Sarah He didn't really say that, did he?

Richard It's what he was thinking though.

Sarah What did he actually say?

Simon We'll be at the summit tomorrow.
Should be fine.

Joe What now?

Simon We get back down.

Joe That's not what I meant.

Simon I know.

Transition to dawn.
  Music.

Sarah So what happened? Did they make it to the top?

Richard About eleven o'clock the next morning.

Simon Chocolate?

Joe Chocolate.

Simon That's the last of the food.

Simon and Joe on the summit.
  They share some chocolate.
  Simon takes photos.

Joe It's getting late. We'd better move.

Richard Things are starting to go wrong
  They're behind schedule
  There's no gas left, so they can't melt snow.
  They're going to have to get down before they
dehydrate.
  They'll have to hurry.
  This is day three.
  Meanwhile, I'm at base camp.
  And I have worries of my own,
  I'm making a fire and gazing at the vast implacable
face of the mountain wondering –
  Who am I? Where am I? What am I?

Sarah Richard.

Richard Sorry.

Sarah Then I don't understand. If they made it to the top, what went wrong?

Surely getting down is the easy bit?

Richard You'd think. But one thing every climber knows is:

Eighty per cent of accidents happen on the descent.
Coming down from the summit was tricky.

Joe climbs, gingerly.
They tried to move fast but soft snow was piled thick along the ridge line.
Very big overhanging cornices.

Joe It's like climbing through shaving foam.

Richard The cornices hung out right out over the west face, if they picked the wrong line they'd step through the snow into couple of thousand feet of emptyness

They walked down slowly, roped together. They had to concentrate. If one of them fell, the other would immediately jump down the other side so they would take each other's weight on either side of the ridge.

Joe (*shouts*) Note to self: Check the descent line next time!

Simon (*shouts*) Note to self: If there is a next time.

Joe Safe!

Simon Safe!

Richard They had thought the ridge ran smoothly all the way down to the col but it didn't –

There was a big notch.

Joe (*shouts*) Shit. Ice cliff. Looks like about a fifty-foot drop.

Richard At base camp, I was making my way along a more philosophical ridge . . .

Joe (*to self*) Balls.

Richard I was reading *Walden* by Henry David Thoreau.

Joe Can't see a way round.

Richard Have you ever read *Walden* by Henry David Thoreau?

Sarah No.

Richard It's quite good.
It's been very useful for my book.

He breaks up the firewood.

Sarah Richard!

Joe sets about climbing down.

Richard Joe couldn't abseil down the notch because the snow at the top was soft and he couldn't find a secure anchor point.
So he decided to climb down.

Sarah Downclimbing is harder than climbing up.

Richard Yes,
You don't have the same ability to see ahead.
And you never know where you're putting your feet.

Joe Fuck.

Gingerly Joe finds a foot placement.

Richard Also the ice was shitty and he was in a hurry.

He breaks a plank of wood.

Joe I'm gonna go I'm gonna go I'm gonna go!

Richard So he fell.

Joe falls.
Joe lands.

Joe screams.
Joe has broken his leg.
A moment.
He realises.
He tests his leg.
Richard breaks more planks into smaller pieces.
Each leg movement makes Joe scream.

Richard In *Walden* by Henry David Thoreau
The author says that to find the truth of ourselves –

Joe Fuck.

Richard We must test ourselves against nature.

Joe Shit.

Richard That it's only by experiencing the wilderness
alone –

Joe Christ!

Richard We discover life –

Joe Hell!

Richard In its purest form.

Joe God!

Richard We find ourselves reflected in the glorious
mirror that is –

Joe Fuuuuuuck.

Richard Nature.

Joe Fuck. Shit. Cock. Piss. Tits.

*Richard takes the splintered guitar and puts it on
the fire.*

Simon Joe?
Joe?

Richard It's really quite profound.

Sarah What happened to Joe?

Richard When Joe fell he hit the steep slope and slid twenty feet into a rock.
    His lower leg drove up – into his knee like this – and smashed it open.
    His thigh fractured near his groin.
    And his ankle was smashed.
    His pineal nerve was crushed.
    Joe can't walk a step, let alone climb.

Simon can see Joe now, though they are at a distance from each other.

Simon What happened?

Joe I fell.

    . . .

Simon You okay?

Joe Leg's broken.

    . . .

Simon Are you sure?

Joe I'm sure.

Simon Wait there.

Joe No worries.

Simon begins to climb down.
    Joe utilises the peanut and some wood planks to demonstrate the situation.

Richard When Joe says 'No worries' . . . that's climber talk for 'Really, a lot of worries.'
    These two men are at nineteen thousand feet.
    With no possibility of rescue.
    On a snow slope this steep and a kilometre high.

Simon can't carry Joe.

And if he even tries to rescue him, he'll probably end up killing himself.

This really is the worst possible situation imaginable. In climbing terms, Joe is basically dead.

Simon is now next to Joe.

Simon Do you want some paracetamol?

Joe Ta.

He takes the pills.
Simon helps Joe get secure on the slope.

Richard If Joe was Simon,
Joe thinks,

Joe I would just leave me here to die, mate.
You don't have to make a big thing of it.
Just say . . . 'Wait here, mate, stay warm. I'll go down and get help.'
I won't make a thing about it.
I promise.
I promise.

Richard He doesn't say it, he doesn't need to.

Simon You secure?

Joe Think so.

A moment.

Simon Fuck! My rope jammed on the abseil down, I'm going to climb back up to free it.

Joe Sure.

Joe takes his rope off.
He is now unmoored.
Simon turns to climb back up.
As he turns he inadvertently knocks Joe . . .

Joe flinches and nearly falls.
He gasps.
A moment.

Simon I won't be long.

Richard Simon free climbed back up the cliff to release the rope.

This was the most dangerous bit of climbing he'd ever done in his life.

Joe has begun to move.
It is agony – but he is doing it.

Joe was moving.

He knew he'd never be able to climb back up.

So he decided to contour across the face of the cliff – along the snow slope.

So he could avoid the notch and reach the ridge.

Where it came lower down.

Joe was unroped, kicking steps into a wall.

On one leg.

If he fell, he was gone.

Simon I watched.

I half wanted him to fall.

Because at least then it would be over.

Richard But he didn't fall.

He kicked and kicked and kicked

And eventually –

Simon Joe!

Joe Simon.

Simon You made it.

Joe I made it.

Richard And this is where things really started to go wrong.

Simon Okay. What we're going to do is this. We're going to get you down.

Joe How?

Simon I'm going to lower you.
   We'll tie our ropes together

Joe What about the knot?

Simon When the knot approaches I'll stop. You take your weight off and tug on the rope to signal you're ready.

Joe Three pulls.

Simon I'll unhook from the belay device, get round the knot and we can go again.

Joe Rope-length by rope-length.

Richard Three thousand foot down.

Sarah How steep?

Richard This steep.
   Constantly swept by wind and spindrift.
   No shelter.
   No anchors.

Joe and Simon looks out at the slope.

Simon No worries.

Richard It's four o'clock.

Joe I don't like the look of the weather.

Simon We could build a snow hole?

Joe We've no gas. We've no water. If we stay here, it'll kill us.

Richard No gas.

You see?

Alpine style. It's beautiful. But it's also dangerous.

Simon What do you think?

Joe Sooner we go, sooner it's over.

Simon There's nothing to hold me on to the hill.

Joe You can dig a bucket seat.

Simon Okay.

Joe Okay.

Richard The plan was this: Simon would anchor himself in the bucket seat, take Joe's weight and lower him. Joe would slide, clattering over the steep ice and rock. His limp leg jagging again and again into the cliff face causing agonising pain.

Simon Ready?

Joe Ready?

Simon Go.

Joe slides off the col on to the face.
Simon lowers.
Joe screams.
Night and storm begin to swirl around him.
Simon joins Richard and Sarah by the campfire.
As they talk, Joe – in photo flashes – experiences the pain of lowering.
There's a stark contrast between the calm campfire and the storm and pain of the night.

Hand over hand.
Simon holds me.
Hand over hand.
He takes my weight.

> *Hand over hand.*
> *The rope burns into me.*
> *Hand over hand.*
> *My leg digs into the snow.*

Joe screams.

Simon Joe?

> *Hand over hand.*
> *The rope is finished.*
> *Simon has to change the knot.*
> *Three pulls on the rope.*
> *I call.*
> *'I'm steady.'*
> *Three pulls back. I brace my weight.*
> *Hand over hand.*
> *Simon holds me.*
> *Hand over hand.*
> *He takes my weight.*
> *The sky is blue.*
> *The mountains white.*

Joe screams.

> *Hand over hand.*
> *Simon holds me.*
> *Hand over hand.*
> *He takes my weight.*
> *Untouched, a blank page*
> *On which we are writing*
> *Together*
> *Hand over hand*
> *An epic poem.*
> *A poem about an epic.*
> *Joe screams.*
> *Hand over hand*
> *And down we go.*
> *Most times you meet an epic poem*

It's a story that's been written
Many hundred years ago
And all you can do
Is try and imagine
What it was like to be the hero.
But what's this now
On Siula Grande?

Joe screams.

What's this now with Si and Jo.
An epic poem
Being written
Right now by us
Here in the snow.
Three tugs on the rope.
'OK GO!'
Hand over hand.
Such bright descending.
Sun on snow and sky in eyes.
Hand over hand.
We're fucking doing it!.
Glacier four thousand –

Joe screams.

                    feet below.
The pain is easy I can take it.
Like swimming in a freezing sea.
The pain is easy, fucking fills me.
I am PAIN and PAIN is ME.

Joe screams.

Cold snow, hot blood, hot rope, cold fear.
We have never been MORE ALIVE.
In rope in snow, we write these five words:
Joe and Simon will survive.

Joe stops sliding.

Simon climbs down to him.

Simon You okay?

Joe (*hiding the pain*) Tip-top. You?

Simon (*hiding the pain*) Tip-top.
  I reckon we might make it.

Joe I reckon we might.

Simon Again?

Joe Again.

Sarah Were you scared?

Simon Incredibly scared.
  From the moment Joe broke his leg
  I could feel death coming to get us both.

Sarah So why didn't you go slower?

Joe flash.

Simon I was also worried Joe would lose consciousness.
If Joe lost consciousness it would all be over.

Joe FUCK!

Simon It wasn't working. My hands were getting stiff
and numb.
  I'd already got frostbite in two fingers.

Sarah Right.

Simon So – it was hard to control the speed.

Richard writes in a notebook.
  Sarah notices.

Sarah What are you doing?

Richard Writing this down for my book.

Joe flash.

Joe FUUUUUUUUUUCK!

Simon lowers.
　　Joe screams.

Shit! SIMON!

Simon He would have felt the cliff coming.

Joe SIMON, STOP!

Simon He probably shouted. I never heard.

Joe SLOW DOWN!

Simon He'd have tried to stop himself going over it. But at that speed he had no chance.
　　He slid over the cliff
　　And out into space.

Joe NO, NO SIMON, STOP!

He dangles in space.

Simon I realised pretty quickly something was wrong.
　　I'd stopped lowering but I wasn't getting three tugs back from Joe.
　　He couldn't take his weight.
　　He'd probably hit an overhang
　　The knot was about ten feet away.
　　But I thought – give him time – maybe he can get himself secure.
　　JOE! JOE!
　　Nothing was happening.
　　JOE!
　　The bucket seat was crumbling.
　　JOE!

Sarah Couldn't he try to climb back up?

Simon His hands were in worse condition than mine.

Joe gives up.

Sarah So what did he do?

Simon What could he do? He just hung in the wind.

Simon How long did he hang for?

Simon An hour and a half.

Sarah And then . . .?

Simon Yes.

A moment.

Sarah How could you do it?

Simon It wasn't emotional. It was practical.

Sarah How could it not be emotional?

Simon Sit here. You be me.

Sarah What?

Simon You be me . . .

Sudden jump to the mountainside –
Sarah is now in the bucket seat.

The rope is pulled taut with the full weight of a man
hanging.

This happens.

It's dark.

This happens.

A storm is raging around you.

This happens.

You haven't eaten or drunk for twenty-four hours.

She weakens.

And frostbite's taking you.

Richard Alpine style.

Sarah Oww fuck!

Simon Okay. What do you know about Joe?

Sarah Joe's on the end of the rope.

Simon Is he alive?

Sarah I think so!

Simon What if he hit his head on a rock? Why is he dangling in the air?

Sarah I can't see. I don't know.

Simon Can you remember the mountain? From when you climbed up? What does it look like?

Sarah I don't know. I wasn't concentrating.

Simon Try to pull him up.

She tries.
  She fails.

You're slipping.

Sarah Shit.

Simon Frostbite's getting worse.

Sarah Joe!

Simon You're going to have to do something.

Sarah Joe!

Simon What are you going to do?

Sarah I'll hold on till morning. At least then we can see.

Simon Morning's eight hours away. You'll be dead by then. The cold will take you.

Sarah Fucking hell! Joe!

Simon He can't hear you.

Sarah I'll walk him down. Kick steps.

Simon Try it –

Sarah JOE!
The rope is slipping!

Simon lowers.

Joe No! Simon! No!

Joe swings upside down.
He tries to right himself.
Joe tries to tie a prusik. His hands are too cold.

Joe gives up, puts his frozen hands together in prayer.

DEAR GOD! YOU UNBELIEVABLE SHIT! WE WERE
DOING SO WELL! YOU FUCK! YOU SHITTY
SHITTY FUCKING SHIT . . .

Shit Shit shit.
Shit.

Joe slumps.

Sarah The knot!

Simon What are you going to do?
What are you going to do?
What are you going to do?

Sarah Shit. Fuck.

Simon Are you going to sit there and die?

Sarah I DON'T HAVE ANOTHER CHOICE!

Simon You have a knife.

A moment.
Sarah cuts the rope.
Joe falls.

Joe screams.
A moment.

It's over.
He's gone.
Let him go.

Simon and Richard leave.

Sarah It's not over.
It's not over.
It's not over till it's over.

Richard This is only halfway.

End of Act One.

Act Two

A gasp.
  Night spins.
  We fall through snow.
  We hit ice.
  Breath leaves our body.
  Dark.
  Stillness for a moment.
  A dull roaring sound – waves on a shingle beach.
  Pulses of white light – flashes.
  Moans and whimpering from the void.
  A head-torch switches on in the dark.
  It picks out Joe.
  He lies crumpled on a ledge.

Joe (*blinded*) Simon? Simon? Simon?

He works himself into a sitting position.

Simon? Is that you? Simon?

Joe switches his head-torch on.
  His head-torch scans the void.
  Emptiness above.
  Emptiness below.
  He looks to the side: Sarah, smoking.

Sarah Hey.

Joe Oh God, it's you!

Sarah Bro.

Joe What are you doing here?

Sarah I heard you were dying
    Inside a crevasse
    I thought I'd come and say goodbye.

Joe You did always like seeing me in pain.

Sarah How are you?

Joe Not brilliant.

Sarah Sorry.

Joe So this is it.

Sarah This is it.

Joe Will you miss me?

Sarah Not really.

Joe Fuck off.

Joe How about you?
    Are you okay?

Sarah Bit mad.

Joe No change there then.

Sarah No change there.

Joe I think I've still got Simon's tobacco.

He finds the tobacco in his rucksack.

Roll us a fag, will you?

Sarah I can't.

Joe My hands are frostbitten to fuck.

Sarah I thought you'd given up.

Joe Come on, sis, I'm dying here.

Sarah I can't roll you a cigarette, Joe, because I'm not really here.

Joe I guess I'll have to roll it myself.

Joe tries to roll the tobacco.
    His hands are too stiff.
    The tobacco falls into the abyss.

Fuck.

Joe laughs.
    Sarah laughs.
    She holds him.
    Simon climbs off the last of the cliff.
    He stops.
    He falls to his knees.

Simon Thank Christ.

He digs a snow hole.

Joe Sal.

Sarah What?

Joe I don't think I'm ready to die.

Sarah I'm not sure you have any other options, bro.

Joe There must be something . . .

Sarah You're the climber?

Joe Up?

Sarah It's an overhanging ice wall.

Joe I can try.

He takes his ice axes.

Sarah Joe.

Tries to kick with his crampons.
    The moves are agony.

Joe.

His feet slip.
  He falls back.
  She falls back.

It's pointless.

Joe I can still try!

Again he tries.
  Again he falls.
  A moment.

Okay . . . sideways. Where does this ledge go?

Sarah Its runs out in both directions.

Joe What about the other side?

Sarah The opposite wall is about twenty feet away.

Joe Fuck, this is a tomb.
  Maybe I can send up a signal?

Sarah What sort of signal?

Joe I don't know – a flare?

Sarah A flare?

Joe laughs.

From your little flare bag?.
  From the little bag of flares all climbers carry around?

Joe I don't know, there must be something.

Sarah Smoke signals?

Joe This is ridiculous.
  SIMON! SIMON! SIMON!

Sarah He won't hear.

Joe He might. He'll be out there looking for me.
  SIIIIIMMOOOOOON!

Sarah He won't hear because he's gone.

Joe What do you mean, gone, he wouldn't leave me.
Unless he was dead.
Maybe he's dead.
He was belaying me.
My weight must have pulled him off the slope.
He'll have slid down the slope and hit his head.
Shit.
But if he's dead then maybe
The weight of his body will act as an anchor on
the rope.
I can use it to prusic up the rope.

Sarah Pull it.

A moment.

Pull the rope.

Joe pulls the rope.
  It falls.
  He sees the rope's end.

Joe He cut it.
Fuck.
He cut the rope.

Silence.
  Wind.
  Simon walks into the camp.
  Richard tends the fire.
  He looks up.
  Simon looks hollow.

Richard Where's Joe?

Simon He's dead.

Richard What happened?

Simon He broke his leg on the hill. We were coming
down. He couldn't walk. Joe was in awful pain. We made
a system. I lowered him. He slid on his bum. Three

hundred feet at a time. We tied the rope together. Sliding
down the hill. Leg bumping off rocks and everything but
It was working. You know. It was working well. We were
doing it. Then a storm came in. Last night. It started
to get hairy. It was just really steep. Joe was suffering.
But we were doing it. I knew we were only two more
lowers away from the glacier and we were going to be
all right . . . and then –

Richard Then what?

Simon I killed him.

Joe Simon killed me.

Sarah No, he didn't.

Joe How else would you describe it?

Sarah You don't know what it was like.

Joe Tell me what it was like, then.

Sarah It was beyond words.

Joe How about these? Rope. Knife. Me. Dead.

Simon I got the end of the rope but it was still taut.

Richard I don't understand.

Simon If Joe had dug in, the rope would go slack. He
would have tugged the rope to say he was secure so
I could climb down. But he didn't. The rope was tight.
All his weight on still on it. So I knew he'd gone over the
edge of a cliff.

Richard Or he was dead.

Sarah You were hanging from a cliff! He was holding
your whole weight on no anchors. He didn't know what
was happening. You could be have been dead for all he

knew. He couldn't hold on to you forever. He didn't even know where you were.

Sarah He knew exactly where I was.

Joe No, he didn't.

Sarah He knew I was on the other end of that fucking rope.

Simon I shouted. But there was no way he could have heard me. I shouted and shouted. But the wind was so strong, the storm was so loud. I listened. I couldn't hear him. I listened. I thought I heard him screaming. But it was probably just the wind. I was slipping. I could feel my strength going. I shouted. I didn't know what to do. I held him.

For an hour and a half.

Richard And all this time Joe was . . .

Simon Hanging.

Sarah All Simon knew is you were hanging over the edge of a cliff. He couldn't lift you up because he didn't have the strength. He couldn't lower you cos there was no rope left.

Joe I could have been hanging ten feet off the ground. He could have walked me down. Cut steps and walked me down to see . . . just to see . . .

Sarah If you were ten feet off the ground then cutting the rope would still have been the right choice. You'd have just dropped to safety. For all he knew you could have been hanging there shouting up to him: 'Cut the rope, Simon, cut the fucking rope.'

Joe But I wasn't.

Richard It must have been awful.

Simon I couldn't hold him.

Joe You do not cut the rope.

Simon I had a knife . . . so –

Joe You just don't do it.

Simon I cut the rope.

Sarah He fought
  All night
  In the cold
  In the ice
  In the dark
  He fought
  He held me
  For as long as he could
  He fought
  Until all his strength was gone.
  What else was he supposed to do?

Joe Die.

Sarah / Simon You / he had no choice.

Joe / Simon There is always a choice.

Sarah / Simon Joe's dead. / You're dead, Joe.

Joe I'm not dead. I'm not.

Sarah Joe, you're on a ledge seventy-five foot down a crevasse. Half your bones are broken. You have no food. You have no water. You've got frostbitten hands. It's minus twenty degrees in here. Outside the wind chill is minus fifty. There is no chance of a rescue. Face it, Joe. You're fucked.

Joe I am not dead.
  There is always a choice
  Until you are dead
  And I am not dead.

Sarah / Joe Yet.

Joe By cutting the rope
Simon gave me a chance.
If I was still on the end of that rope
I'd have died like Toni Kurz.
Frozen and helpless and alone
But I'm not dead
I'm here.
Simon gave me a chance.

Sarah Joe?
What are you doing?

Joe I'm looking for an ice screw.

Sarah Why?

Joe I'm going to clip the rope to it and descend.

Sarah Where to?

Joe Down there.

Sarah You're going to descend into that?

Joe Yup.

Sarah But there's nothing down there.
It's hell
It's bottomless.

Joe Simon gave me a chance
But it's not a chance unless I take it.
And I can't take it lying here.

Sarah But what if the rope runs out before you reach the bottom?

Joe I'll drop.

Sarah Jesus, Joe.

Joe It's all right, sis.

There is always a choice.
And this is mine.

Joe lowers himself into the darkness.
   He fades.
   Heartbeat.
   Breath.
   Pain.
   Then silence.
   After it has been silent for so long, we wonder if there's been a lighting malfunction . . .
   Silence for just a little longer.
   Until –

Richard picks out a song, carefully, and slightly wrongly, on the guitar.
   'May You Never' by John Martyn.
   As he sings
   Simon takes off his climbing clothes.
   He moves, slowly, bruised.
   He folds his clothes up, and lays them carefully on a table.
   After some time:

Simon Richard . . .

Richard Mm?

Simon Can you not?

And then, shouted from the void.

Joe Sis?
   Sis?
   SIS!

Sarah Joe, is that you?

Joe It's me.

Sarah I thought you were dead.

Joe No.
   Sis
   Look
   Light.

Sarah I know!
   Isn't it glorious.
   I'm up here on glacier and the sun's coming up.

   Light.
      A thin shaft in the darkness, but it's there and it
   grows
      Until it illuminates . . . the floor.
      Sarah looks around.
      She's in the centre of a huge circular bowl of
   mountains.
      Sun, snow, creak of glacier, high peaks, stone-fall.

There's bloody mountains everywhere.
   You should see it!

Joe I think this might be the bottom of the crevasse.
   There's a snow slope over there which goes up towards
the light.
   It might be a way out
   I think it's a way out.

Sarah Great. Hurry up and get out of there. You're
missing the sunrise.

   Joe falls to his knees.

This calls for a tune.

   Sarah clicks her fingers.
      Music: 'This is the Day'.

Joe Wait, sis . . . Shit . . .

Sarah What?

Joe The floor isn't solid.
   Jesus.
   Sis!

Sarah What now?

Joe The floor –
   It might give way.

Sarah So?

Joe It's just a snow bridge.

Sarah So, snow bridge is better than no bridge, isn't it?

Joe I can see dark patches.

Sarah Just hurry up and get across so we can have fun
in the sun.

Joe Christ, I can hear snow falling below me.
   Maybe if I spread my weight.

Gingerly, Joe attempts to cross the bridge.

Sarah So many mountains.
   You know, when I imagined this place, I thought it
would be like the Lake District or something, you know,
just scenery . . .
   But it's not is it?
   These mountains go right up to the fucking sun.
   I mean it actually takes your breath away.
   JOE!

Joe Shit! Sis, don't shout,

Sarah JOE!

Joe You'll disturb the snow.

Sarah I'M SAYING IT TAKES YOUR BREATH AWAY!

Joe Christ.

Sarah Yerupaja, Siula Grande, Siula Chico –
Isn't that the cliff you fell down?
I mean it's like the side of a block of flats.
When Simon said 'cliff' I imagined, you know, a cliff –
But when you see it.
Jesus.
How the hell did you survive that?
Joe –
What's keeping you?

Joe It's just very very dangerous, sis.

Sarah I want breakfast.
We could be having a cup of tea and a bacon roll if we had bacon or a roll or tea . . . or a cup.
Still.
Sitting here in the lovely warm sun's the next best thing.
Come on!

Joe makes it across the snow bridge.

Joe (*to self*) Thank Christ.
I've made it, sis! I've made it to the snow slope!

Sarah Finally.

Joe Shit.

Sarah What now?

Joe It's just this looks really steep.

Sarah Maybe don't look at it then.

Joe (*to self*) I'll have to – maybe if I – damn – or if I –

Sarah What are you going to eat first?

Joe It must be about fifty feet.

Sarah When we get back to camp.

Joe I'm going to have to pull myself up on my arms.

Sarah I think I'm going to have beans.

Joe groans.

Just a big bowl of beans.

Joe groans.

A big bowl of beans and buttered white bread to dip in it.

Joe falls back.

Grated cheese on top.

Joe (*to self*) This is ridiculous.

Sarah Bit of ham.

Joe climbs again.
Groans again.

Sarah Twix.

Joe groans.

After Eight.

Joe groans.

Joe? Joe?
 What are you doing down there?
 Having a party?
 You've been at it for five hours.
 It's nearly lunchtime.
 I thought you were supposed to be a climber.

Joe I am, sis.
 This is just really, really difficult.

Sarah The sun's too warm.
 I'm feeling sleepy.
 Give me a shout if you make it out alive.

Joe reaches the light.
  He hatches into life
  Like a chick exiting an egg.
  He revels in the sensations of light and air.

Joe I made it.
  I made it.
  I made it.

She helps him to his feet.

I'M NOT DEAD!

Sarah embraces him, holds him up.
  He touches her face – hugs her.

I'M NOT DEAD, SIS! WHOOOOOO!
  I'M ALIVE!

His voice echoes all around the mountains.

Sarah It's a good feeling, isn't it?

Joe It's a great feeling.

Sarah Shame it can't last.

She knees him in the balls.

It's a good feeling, isn't it?

Joe It's a great feeling.

Sarah Shame it can't last.

She knees him in the balls.

Joe Owwwww! What did you do that for?

Sarah It's not me, bro, it's your leg.
  Every time you stand up you put weight on your
crushed nerve.
  It's not personal, you just forgot.

She lets him drop.
Joe curls up on the ground, groaning.

Okay.
You're alive.
Being alive is a good start.
But there's still a long way to go.
How long have you got?

Joe It's morning. Simon will be getting back to camp around now. He'll probably sleep, take a day to recover, pack, then go.

Sarah So, you've got two days.

Joe Two days to cover eight miles.

Sarah Piece of piss.

Joe Sis, I can't walk.

Sarah takes out a stop watch.
And a bag of peanuts.
A digital clock appears above the pub.

Sarah Okay, Joe, so this is where you are.

Sarah places a peanut on the floor.

Here's base camp.

Sarah places a pint glass on the floor.

In between is –

Joe A glacier.

Sarah The glacier looks like –

Joe A motorway after an earthquake.

Sarah Oh my God.
Smashed ice broken up with hundred-foot deep crevasses –

72

Sarah draws this pattern on the chalk board.

Joe It's suicidal to cross a glacier alone.

Sarah Not as suicidal as staying here.
Besides, you've got me.

Joe If I could stand I could use my height to look ahead and see the safest route.

Joe tries to stand up.
Sarah hits Joe's leg with an ice-axe handle.

Sarah Well, that's not going to work, is it?

Joe No.

Sarah So, let's see: you're broken, you've got no food or drink, you're dehydrated, hypothermic, hungry and in shock . . . plus you're exhausted after two nights of what can only be described as less than ideal conditions –

Joe Hell.

Sarah And now you have to find a way through a maze.

Joe That's about the size of it.

Sarah So, what's the plan?

Joe Crawl.

Sarah Perfect.
Easy.
Crawl.
Which way?

Joe makes a random choice.

Joe That way.

Sarah Okay. Go.

Joe begins to crawl.
Sarah traces his progress.
Joe comes to a stop.

Sarah Why are you stopping?

Joe Crevasse.

Sarah hits him.

Sarah Jesus Christ, you shitting idiot.

Joe Owww.

Sarah You made the wrong choice.
You're just going to have to go back.

Joe crawls back in the other direction.

This is going to be awful.

Joe Blocked.

She hits him again.

Sarah Where now?

*Unwilling to make another wrong choice,
Joe forces himself to stand in order to see.
It's really hard.*

Joe Owww . . . God . . . Jesus!

He makes it to his feet.

Sarah What?

Joe The glare off the glacier.

She swings a light right into his eyes.

Sarah Don't you have sunglasses?

Joe Crushed them in the fall.

She puts her own sunglasses on.

Sarah Oh, that's annoying.

Joe squints – it's hard to see but . . .

Can you see a way forward?

Joe No.
  Wait.

Sarah What?

Joe Footprints.
  In the snow.

Sarah Footprints.

Joe Look.

Sarah A yeti?
  Oh God, please don't let it be a yeti.
  The last thing you need right now is a mauling from a man-bear.

Joe It's not a yeti.
  It's Simon.
  He bivvied here last night.
  He must have walked out this morning.
  All I need to do is follow his footprints and I'll find a way through.

Sarah Brilliant.

Joe Brilliant.

  She whacks his leg again.

Sarah You know what, Joe?
  I have a feeling this is going to be fun.
  I have a feeling this is going to be a fucking breeze.

  Joe slide-crawls following Simon's footprints.
    They watch Joe crawl . . . agonisingly . . .
    The clock whizzes down by five hours.

Joe Made it.

Sarah You made it. Well done!
  Now you just need to cross the moraines.
  Four miles of rock and ice and stones

All piled up in heaps.
Like someone's emptied out a massive bag of Lego
All across the kitchen floor.

Joe I can't slide over rocks.

Sarah You can hop.

Joe Hop?

Sarah On one leg.
It's going to be tricky but –

Joe Tricky! It's going to be fucking impossible!

Sarah It'll be fine.

Joe My leg is smashed!

Sarah For goodness sake, Joe!
It's all glass half-empty with you.
One leg is smashed
The other isn't.
Look, you've have had easier walk-outs from a hill.
But the sun is shining and you've got me.
You can do it.

Joe How?

Sarah You're just going to break it down into achievable tasks.

Joe All right.

Sarah So what's the first task?

Joe Learn how to walk.

Joe opens up his rucksack.
He lays out his kit.
Joe uses his Karrimat and rucksack straps to make a basic leg splint.
Sarah watches.

Sarah This is good.
Improvisation, I like it.
This is all good.

With the Karrimat as a makeshift splint, Joe stands.

Joe Lift. Brace. Hop.

*Joe places his axe, lifts the bad foot forward, brace,
hop.*
She smashes his leg.
Agony.
He falls over.
He whimpers.
He gets up.
He places the axe . . .

Lift brace hop.

She smashes his leg.
This time he doesn't fall.
Takes the pain.

Sarah See, I don't know what you were moaning about.

Joe Lift brace hop!

Sarah Lift brace hop!

A moment of triumph.

Joe Sarah?

Sarah Yes.

Joe How long is it since I've had anything to drink?

Sarah I don't know, it's your mouth.
Three days? – No – two days, three nights.

Joe A person needs half a litre of water a day just to stay
alive.
If I don't get water very soon I'll die.

Sarah Eat some snow.

Joe It doesn't work like that. I can't get enough water from snow. You need a massive amount of snow just to get a teaspoon of water. If I eat it I'll just end up hypothermic.

Sarah Wasn't there a little puddle at Bomb Alley?

Joe I won't reach it tonight.

Sarah You might.

Joe There's no way.
    Fuck, sis.
    I'm going to die.
    I'm going to die from dehydration.

He gives up.

Sarah Dehydration?
    That doesn't seem very glamorous.
    Not very Toni Kurz.
    Still, it's up to you.
    If it's dehydration you want, dehydrate away, feel free.
    I won't stop you.
    I mean, I'm all right – I've got my Evian.

She swigs from a water bottle.

Joe I don't have a choice.

Sarah There is always a choice.
    Until you are dead.
    And you are not dead yet –

Joe Yet.

Sarah Bomb Alley is four and a half miles away.
    Four and a half miles in one day equals two hundred and twenty feet every per hour,
    Take out four hours for rest.

That means
You need to make roughly three hundred feet forward progress every hour.

Joe Shut up, shut up, shut up! I can't think of that. It's too much, it's too big.

Sarah So what are you going to think about?

Joe That rock.

Sarah Which rock? There's hundreds of them!

Joe The one shaped like a dying elephant, do you see it?
I see it.

Sarah Nothing else.
Forget everything else.
All you have to do is get to that rock in half an hour.
Go!

Joe Lift, brace, hop . . .

Repeats six more times.
Sarah sets the stopwatch going again.
Water drip sounds.
Rock and stonefall.
After a while –

Sarah God this is boring.
I wonder what's on the telly.

Sarah switches on the pub telly.
Wogan . . .

Terry Wogan Hello and welcome to *Wogan*!
And now a guest who doesn't need any introduction.
Yorkshire climber Joe Simpson. This is the eejit who fell off a mountain when his friend murdered him. Then he only went and crawled over two miles of old chairs.
I'd have thought that was awful sore. But did it matter?
No – he ended up dead of deyhydration. What a prat!

Sarah switches channels.

Joe Aim for the elephant.
Made it!

Sarah switches the pub telly channel.

Sarah Twenty-nine minutes and seventeen seconds.

Joe Easy. Where next?

Sarah Stone shaped like a dancing nun.
Go!

Joe crawls again.
The clock speeds forward.

David 'Kid' Jensen Here's Legs and Co doing the brand new dance – lift brace hop – it's in all the discos now where the kids dance it in honour of 'Dead' Joe Simpson, the climber who danced his way down an Andean Glacier. Lift brace hop – lift brace hop – try it – you can do it at home.

All three of them do the lift-brace-hop along with Joe.

All Lift-brace-hop! Lift-brace-hop!

Sarah switches the telly off.
Static.
Heat. Sun. Glare.

Joe Made it!
I can hear water.

Sarah It's little rivers running under the glacier.

Joe It's only a few feet away.
I can smell it.

Sarah But you can't reach it.

She drinks some Evian from her bottle.

Joe I am so thirsty.

She dips her finger in the water.
She runs her wet finger along his lips.
He tries to rest.
She holds his head in her hands.
Antiques Roadshow *on the telly.*

Arthur Negus Now what have we here? Do you know what this is, madam?

Lady I think it's the skull of Joe Simpson.

Arthur Negus It is! It is the skull of long-lost climber Joe Simpson. Do you mind telling us . . . how did it come to be in your possession?

Lady Well, it's a funny story. My husband and I were trekking in Peru one day when a condor flew down and dropped it right in front of me. I knew it was Joe Simpson because of his mummified face. The bird must have found him on a glacial moraine and just picked the flesh off his bones.

Arthur Negus That's exactly right, madam. It is the skull of long lost climber Joe Simpson!
Do you have any idea how much it's worth?

Lady Oh I couldn't say. We'd never sell it anyway.

Arthur Negus Well, you don't often get mountaineers' skulls on the market. And this one is in very good condition so – if I were you, I would insure Joe Simpson's skull for . . . five pounds.

Gasp from the crowd.

Lady As much as that!

Joe You cow.

Sarah You love it, Joe, you always did.

Joe Next rock.

With each rock, she tortures him.

Sarah Sick dog
   Shitting Hitler
   Two sad hens
   Thatcher's forehead
   Taj Mahal
   Small Ben Nevis
   Unwashed dishes
   Skull
   Cross
   Coffin.

He stops.
   Sarah beats Joe's leg hard, a number of times, with the pool cue.

Coffin
   Coffin
   Coffin.

Joe Stop!

She stops.

How long do I have to go?

Sarah It doesn't matter.

Joe Tell me.

Sarah No.
   Next rock.
   Nothing else.
   Half an hour
   Coffin.
   GO!

He recovers.
   He gets up.

He goes.
Sarah switches the telly over to another channel.
Legs and Co do 'Brown Girl in the Ring' on Top of
the Pops.

Sarah Oh, I like this one.

She sings along.

'Brown girl in the ring, tra la la la la,
There's a brown girl in the ring, tra, la la la la la . . .'

Joe Don't.

Sarah What?

Joe Don't sing that.

Sarah Why not?

Joe Sing something else.

Sarah You're the DJ, bro, what would you like me to
sing.

Joe I don't know. Just not that.

Sarah
'Brown girl in the ring, tra la la la la
She looks like a sugar in a plum tra la.'

Joe If you have to sing, at least sing something I actually
like.

Sarah Like what?

Joe
'There's a lady who knows all that glitters is gold
And she's climbing the stairway to heaven . . .'

Sarah
BROWN GIRL IN THE RING, TRA LA LA LA LA.

Joe What about the blues?

Sarah *BROWN GIRL IN THE RING*

Joe Sarah, I'm crawling across broken rocks a thousand miles from home,
   The least you could do is sing me the blues.

Sarah *TRA LA LA LA LA LA*

Joe What about something classical? Put some classical music in my head. Think of something classical.

   She thinks.

Sarah No.
   You need something jolly, Joe.
   Some jolly music to crawl to.
   This is perfect.
   All together now –
   Simon and Richard!

   Brown girl in the ring – tra la la la la
   There's a brown girl in the ring – tra la la la la la
   Brown girl in the ring – tra la la la la
   She looks like a sugar in a plum
   Tra la!

Joe I should've stayed in the fucking crevasse.

Sarah Come on!

Joe Don't encourage them.

   Show me a motion tra la la la
   I said show me a motion
   Tra la la la la la
   Show me a motion
   Tra la la la la
   She looks like a sugar in a plum
   Tra la!

Joe Made it.

He falls.

Sarah Thirty minutes.

Joe I hate you.

Sarah If you don't like the music, Joe.
Go faster.
Faster you go, sooner it's over.
Rock like a sick cow.
Go.

On television: Tom Paulin and Germaine Greer.

Paulin My name is Tom Paulin. Hello and welcome to
Tom Paulin goes into Death where tonight we're
discussing 'Brown Girl in the Ring', the song which is
filling the head of Joe Simpson as his life ebbs away in the
high Andes. To discuss it I have with me my usual guest,
Germaine Greer.

Applause.

Germaine, what did you make of it?

Greer What I want to know is why is the brown girl in
the bloody ring anyway!?

She hits Joe.

Paulin They sing 'She looks like a sugar in a plum', so is
it some kind of a jam ring?

Greer Is she supposed to be an acrobat?

Paulin Why is she supposed to show him a motion?

Greer hits Joe.

Is it a bowel motion?

Greer Surely not.

She hits Joe.

I have a theory.

Paulin What's your theory, Germaine?

Greer What if it's not 'Show me A-motion'? What if it's 'Show me E-motion'?

What if the song is saying to Joe Simpson: 'Show me Emotion.'

She hits Joe.

And of course – Joe Simpson can't show emotion.
Not now.
Not at this moment.

She hits Joe.

Because if he does –

She hits Joe.

Paulin He'll break down crying and he won't stop till he's dead!

Joe close to breaking.

Both Tra la!

Paulin Join us next week on *Tom Paulin goes into Death* to discuss amongst other things the new best selling memoir that's taking the climbing world by storm, *Avoiding the Touch*, by Richard I-Don't-Know-His-Second-Name.

Theme music.

Joe NO!

Joe collapses.
He laughs.
Laughs and laughs.

Sarah Did you make it?

Joe Missed it by three minutes.

Sarah No you didn't.

Joe I've been late for the last five rocks.

Sarah No you haven't.

Joe Yes I have.

Sarah You made them all.

Joe It's getting late.

Sarah It's still early.

Joe I'm tired.

Sarah You're fine.

Joe collapses to rest.
    Sarah finds a handful of gravel.
    She pours some water over it.
    She puts the wet gravel in an ashtray.

Oh Joe, Joe! Look! Good news!

Joe What? What is it?

Sarah We're at Bomb Allley!
    Damp sand!
    Some of the surface snow must have melted in the sun.
    It's puddled in some gravel.

Joe laughs.

Water.

*She puts the ashtray on the floor just out of Joe's
reach.*
    Joe crawls to the ashtray.
    He puts the stones in his mouth.
    He sucks them.

87

Now.
Rock shaped like a country church in Yorkshire.
Three hundred feet.
Half an hour.
Go.

Joe crawls.

Not far now.
You're past Bomb Alley.
The lake's not far away.
If you keep up the pace you'll be there by dawn.

Joe It's a beautiful night.

He rests on Sarah's lap.

Sarah Only the scree and the river-bed left.

Joe digs into his rucksack.

What are you looking for?

Joe Sleeping bag.

Sarah No – Joe . . .
Edge of the lake.
One hour.
Go.

Joe doesn't move.

You need to keep going, Joe.

Joe has made a pillow made of his own jacket.

Sarah Don't get comfortable.

Joe I am so far away from comfortable, sis.
I need to rest
For a moment.
Rest, little nap, gather my strength, then go again.

Sarah Joe –

She raises the pool cue.

Joe Please.
Don't hurt me.
Please don't hurt me any more.

Sarah Okay.

She lowers the cue.

Just for a moment.

He takes off his boots.
She helps him.
Sarah sees Joe's feet.
Purple, livid, horrific.

Oh my God.
Christ.
It's disgusting.
It's so swollen!
So fucking hot.

Joe I'm never going to walk again.

She touches his feet.
He screams.

Sarah Sorry.

Joe It's okay.

He starts to get into his sleeping bag.

Sarah What are you doing?

Joe I just need to sleep.

Sarah No!

She fights him.

No sleep.
You have to move.
Move now, rest later.

Joe There's no point.

He points to the clock.

It's too late.
   Simon's gone.
   He'd have got back yesterday. He rested then he
packed. There was no reason for him to stay. Richard
would have been desperate to leave. He thought he was
off for an interesting trek on his gap year and then he
got mixed up in a mountaineering tragedy. They'd have
left this afternoon.

She tries to rouse him, but he's fading.

Sarah What if they didn't?

Joe They did.

Sarah There's barely half a mile to go.
   If it was light you could see them.
   Just break it down into achievable tasks.

Joe What if I crawl all night
   And get there just after dawn.
   Call out into the mist
   And no one answers back?
   What if I crawl on
   And see flattened grass where the tents had been.
   Feel the warmth of them still on the ground.
   What about that, sis,
   The loneliness of that.
   What then?

Sarah We go on.

Joe No.
   Too slow.
   Too late.
   It's over.

Sarah Joe.

She hits him.

Joe.

He doesn't react.

Joe.

She hits him again.

Joe.

He doesn't move.
    Hit.
    Shake.
    Hit.
    She stops.

Joe Simpson, if you die here
    I'll fucking kill you.

Simon stands by a fire.
    He burns Joe's clothes.
    Richard brings Simon a cup of cocao.

Richard What are you doing?

Simon Burning Joe's clothes.

Richard I've packed his tent.
    We can sell it in the market in Lima.
    What about the rest of his stuff?

Simon Some notebooks, a couple of paperbacks, not much else.

Richard He must have been keeping a diary.

Simon I didn't read it.

Richard This seems to be a letter to somebody.
    Sarah?

Simon Just put it inside the book.

Richard Okay.

They watch the flames.

How are you feeling?

Simon All right.

Richard I mean how are you feeling about leaving?
   If we're going to go before it gets dark
   We should start packing up.

Simon We can't go.

Richard Why?

Simon I can't find his money.

Richard What?

Simon Before we left, Joe hid his wallet.
   A hundred dollars. Under a rock
   He showed it to me.
   I can't find it.

Richard Have you looked?

Simon Of course I've looked.
   All the rocks look the fucking same to me.
   I wasn't really concentrating when he showed me.
   I didn't think it was information I would have to
remember.
   I was expecting him to come back.

Richard It's only a hundred dollars.

Simon It's Joe's money.

Richard I know but it's only –

Simon It's Joe's.
   I'll find it.

I just need to keep turning over stones.
We'll go tomorrow

Joe crawls.
  Night falls.
  Stars.
  Light wind.
  Gentleness.
  Joe reaches a rock.

Sarah Made it.

Joe . . .

Joe curls up in his sleeping bag.
  The clock stops.
  And we are in the pub.
  The Clachaig Inn, one evening in summer.
  Richard puts money in the jukebox. Etta James:
'*I'd Rather Go Blind'.*
  A golden sun shines in through the pub window.
  Richard sits at a table reading climbing books and
writing notes.
  Joe enters the pub, dressed in civvies, jeans and a
T-shirt.
  He is stiff and sore, but better . . . no longer in
horrible pain.
  He looks at the body in the curled-up worm of the
sleeping bag, himself.
  He looks at Sarah.
  At Richard reading.
  Richard notices him.

Richard Joe!
What are you doing here?

Joe Dying.

Richard Mate.
Sit down.

Joe sits.

How are you?
Stupid question.
Do you want a pint?

Joe doesn't respond.
  He picks up Richard's book.

I'm reading all about Toni Kurz and the Eiger. It's such
a compelling story. Four young men – a new breed
Together they invent Alpine climbing. Young and bold,
they make an attempt on mighty North Face. The whole
world watches, and then: disaster!
  Have you ever heard of it?

Joe nods.

Reading it, I keep thinking about you. A young man
hanging on the end of a rope. Trying and trying and
trying to survive but in the end . . . he can't . . . So near
and yet so far.
  I keep thinking how lonely that must feel.
  Did it feel lonely?

Joe Yes.

Richard 'Lonely'.

He writes 'lonely' in his notebook.

Is this you?

Joe Yes.

Richard When they find you, that's how you'll be. All
curled up in your sleeping bag, as if you've just fallen
asleep. You look peaceful.
  Is it peaceful?

Joe Yes.

Joe 'Peaceful'.

He writes 'peaceful' in his notebook.
They all look at the curled worm of a man in a bag.
Simon enters, carrying a pint.

Joe Si.

Simon Joe.

Joe I'm sorry.

Simon It's all right.

Joe I tried.
I really really tried.
But –

Joe / Richard Ich kann nicht mehr.

Simon puts the pint down.

Joe Is that for me?

He sits . . . He strokes the cool glass of beer.

I'm so fucking thirsty.

Joe goes to hold the pint.

Sarah Don't drink it.

She knocks the pint over, out of his hands.

Joe Jesus, sis!
It's not poison.
Don't take it so seriously.
It's just the oxygen leaving my brain.
When the oxygen leaves your brain you get great
dreams.
I always wondered what mine would be like.
Turns out it's the Clachaig on a summer night.
Heaven.

Sarah It's ironic, isn't it?

Joe What is?

Sarah Well,
This would make such a good story.
Siula Grande.
Rope, glacier, crawl, dreams.
Round the table at the Clachaig.
A real epic.
But the only person who can really tell the tale is going to be dead.

Richard Hello?

Sarah Fuck off, Richard.

Joe It's all right. Richard can tell the story.

Richard *Avoiding the Touch:*
An Incredible Story of Survival.

Sarah It isn't a story of survival, Richard, if the hero didn't fucking survive.

Richard But he did survive?

Sarah What?

Simon He means me.

A moment.

Sarah For fuck's sake, no! Joe!

She slaps him.

Wake up!

Slap.

Wake up!

Slap.

Wake up!

He just smiles, beatific.

Sarah Why won't you fight!

Richard Honestly, if I were in Joe's position, I'd have given up long ago.

Sarah You wouldn't.

Richard I would.

Sarah You only think you would because it's not your life you're thinking about.
　　It's his life.
　　And you don't value his life as much as your own.

Richard I just mean –

Sarah You might be a nerd, Richard, but you're still an animal
　　And when the light's fading
　　You would fight.
　　Fight with every ounce of strength you have.

Richard Fight what?

Sarah Death.

Joe 'Ay, but to die –'

Sarah What?

Joe Shakespeare.
　　Our English teacher made me learn it at school as a punishment for smoking.

Simon 'Ay, but to die, and go we know not where' –

Joe You know it?

Richard It's from *Measure for Measure*.

Joe / Simon
　　'Ay but to die . . . and go we know not where.
　　The weariest and most loathèd worldly life

That age, ache, penury and imprisonment
Can lay on nature is a paradise
To what we fear of death.'

Joe I can't believe you know that.

Simon I don't. You do.

Joe laughs.

Joe When do I get found?

Simon Next climbing season.

Richard You'll be dry as dust by then.

A moment.

Simon All right, well
I suppose we'd better –

Richard Let you get on.

Joe Sure.

Richard Really nice to have met you, Joe.

Joe Yeah.

Simon See you, mate.

Joe See you.
Sis?

Opens his arms for a hug.
She refuses the hug.

The funny thing is, sis, after everything else
This bit
The actual dying
Feels surprisingly
Nice.

He goes to lie down.
Sarah suddenly grabs him.

Sarah No.

She holds Joe's body off the floor.

You're not gone.
  Not yet.

Won't let him lie down.

You're still warm
  There's still heat
  Still breath, Joe
  Still life.
  Don't go.
  Live.
  You have to live.

Joe Why?

Sarah Why?

A moment.
  In a repeat of the sequence when Simon showed her how to climb, Sarah manipulates Joe's body . . .
  As she speaks, she conjures.

To feel
  to rest your arm on a wooden table
  drink a pint
  roll a fag
  watch the dust dancing in the sunlight
  daydream
  hear people talking in a Yorkshire accent
  smell a woman's perfume as she passes
  listen to a song
  touch skin
  dance
  lose yourself.
  Life, Joe . . .

She cannot hold him.

He curls up.

Life if you have it, you have to live it.

Joe Why?

A moment . . .

Sarah Because it's there.

Joe is gone.
    The pub is empty.
    Sarah, alone at a table, she has the polythene bag
with Joe's possessions.
    She lights a cigarette.
    She opens the letter.
    She reads.

Sarah 'Dear Sarah,

'If you're reading this letter there must have been some
kind of a fuck-up.

'So the first thing I want to say is, "Sorry."

'I'm writing this sitting on a rock in the Huayhuash
mountain range at the foot of a mountain called Siula
Grande in what we laughingly call "base camp". It's
basically two tents and a hippy called Richard who wears
clown trousers and plays the guitar. Two things which,
as you know, I do not like. Nevertheless, Richard has
agreed to watch our tents for days while we're away
climbing. You know me. Always doing things on a wing
and a prayer. Fuck it.'

. . .

'Despite what everyone says. I don't have a death wish.
I very much did not mean to be dead so . . . I'm sorry.'

. . .

'I know you don't really get climbing
I know you think it's dumb
But I want you to know
I love it

Really
It brings me joy.'

. . .

'As I write this letter to you, snow is falling, dampening
the writing paper. I'm settling down for a fag, a brew and
a sleep. I just came back from a shit. The latrine's up
among a rockfall about a hundred yards from the tent.
You sit on a stone and you look out over a view of
mountains and valleys stretching for miles. Clouds below
you. Birds below you. It's the most beautiful khazi in the
world. And as I squatted there laying a cable I just started
laughing – I'm on top of the fucking world –'

. . .

'So, I'm sorry I'm dead
I really am, sis,
But I want you to know.
I died laughing
On top of the fucking world.
Your brother
Joe.'

Sarah scrunches up the letter and throws it in the bin.
  She leaves.
The pub fades away.
We are alone now, under the stars
On the cold of the rocks
Wind and stone.
A man dead in a bag.
Snow falls on him.
A moment
A breath
A breath again – stronger
A third breath.

Joe Aaaaaaay!
  Ay!

He straightens his body.

He pulls himself out of the sleeping bag.
This is a superhuman effort.

But.

He lifts himself into a crawling position.

To.

He crawls forward.

Die.

Every movement hurts him.

Ay.

He lifts himself.

But.

Every word a gasp of pain.

To.

He gains in power.

Die.

This is his last hurrah.

AY!

He falls.
He hits his head.
He rises.

But.

A further crawl.

To.

A pause, a fall.

Die.

Ay but to die ay but to die ay but to die ay but to die

Shit
Shit
God.

He realises he has shit on his hands.

Human shit.
Shit
Human shit
Is so beautiful.

Joe slumps.
He makes a voiceless cry.
He tries so hard to make a voiced cry.
But it is voiceless.
He tries another cry.
Another cry.
He slumps.
The camp, night.
The sound of wind and water.
A head-torch comes on.

Richard Simon.

. . .

Simon.

Simon Mm?

Richard Did you hear something?

Simon No.

A pause.

Richard I thought I heard something.

A moment.

It sounded like a voice.

Simon It's the wind.

Richard It was calling.

Simon What did it say?

Richard It didn't say anything, as such, it was more –
. . .

He makes a sound like a distant, voiceless, cry . . .

Simon Okay.

Richard makes a sound like a distant, voiceless, cry again.

Richard, you're in the mountains, there's been an accident, you're going to hear ghosts. It happens all the time.

Richard Does it?

Simon You get thoughts, they mix up with the noises of the hill and you think you hear people calling . . . but there's no one there . . . It's just the wind.

Richard Yeah.

A moment.

Simon Richard. Do you mind putting your torch off? We need to sleep.

Richard Oh. Yeah. Sorry.

Simon Spinoza's coming with the donkeys at six.

Richard Yeah. Yeah. Sorry.

Richard switches his head-torch off.
    A moment.
    The wind.
    A head-torch comes on again.
    Simon opens up the tent.
    He climbs out.
    His head-torch scans the darkness.
    Nothing . . .

And then . . . he finds him.
A monstrous, broken figure, standing . . . hands
outstretched.

Joe Help me
Help me

Joe totters.

Please.

Simon quickly moves forward and catches him.
Simon holds Joe.
Richard emerges from the tent.
Richard's light catches them both.

The End.